# under one olive tree
## Jews and Gentiles Grafted In

# Dawn Rose Brekke
# Renee Grace

authorHOUSE®

AuthorHouse™
1663 Liberty Drive
Bloomington, IN 47403
www.authorhouse.com
Phone: 1 (800) 839-8640

Published by AuthorHouse    04/20/2015

ISBN: 978-1-5049-0298-4 (sc)
ISBN: 978-1-5049-0296-0 (hc)
ISBN: 978-1-5049-0297-7 (e)

Print information available on the last page.

**This book is dedicated to my Lord and Savior-
Jesus the Messiah,**
And to my dear brother, Dr. Dean Sousa.
Dean, may you always rest between
the shoulders of Adonai.

### _Zechariah: 8:23:_

_This is what the Lord Almighty says: In those days ten men from all languages and nations will take firm hold of one Jew by the edge of his robe and say, "Let us go with you, because we have heard that God is with you."_

### _Galatians 3:26-29:_

_"You are all sons of God through faith in Christ Jesus, for all of you who were baptized into Christ have clothed yourselves with Christ. There is neither Jew nor Greek, slave nor free, male nor female, for you all belong to Christ, then you are Abrahams' seed, and heirs according to the promise."_

## <u>Acknowledgements:</u>
We would like to thank our Messianic Rabbis for serving Yeshua Ha Mashiach, bringing brothers and sisters, Jewish and Gentile Messianic Believers together as one family, under one Olive Tree. Thanks to Phyllis Rosiner and Marie Jackson for Assisting to proof read this book. We are all believers in Yeshua and we are all one.

## <u>Our Rabbis:</u>
Rabbi Loren Jacobs & Rabbi Glen Harris, Oakland County, Michigan; John and Marcia Glueck, Kansas City, Missouri; Rabbi Judah Ungerman and Jim Pickins, Ft. Myers, Florida:

We would like to acknowledge and thank our parents for bringing us up in the faith in Yeshua. Agape love to our family in Yeshua.

**Thank you to Yeshua Ha Mashiach For our salvation and His Love and Sacrifice He paid for us to be guaranteed Eternal life! Much Love to the Ruach Ha Kodesh, our Counselor and present witness of Yeshua Ha Mashiach.**

## <u>*God predestined us to be His sons:*</u>

*Ephesians 1:4-8: For He chose us in Him before the creation of the world to be holy and blameless in His sight. In love, He predestined us to be adopted as His sons through Jesus Christ (Yeshua), in accordance with His pleasure and will, to the praise of His glorious grace, which He has freely given us in the One He loves. In Him, we have redemption through His Blood, the forgiveness of sins, in accordance with the riches of Gods' grace that He lavished on us with all wisdom and understanding.*

# *With Just a Whisper*

With just a whisper I called your name
And you as my child were considered the best.
With just a whisper your sins were made
As far as the East is from the West.
With just a whisper I formed the earth,
With just a whisper
You came forth in birth.
With just a whisper the birds began to sing.
With just a whisper I sent an offering.
With just a whisper my Son Gave His Life,
To free you from anguish, to end all the pain.
With just a whisper
You were cleansed anew,
Listen my child
To what I am saying to you.
Now try to imagine me speaking
What indeed that could do.
But remember it is just a whisper
When I say,

**"I Love You."**

# When He Calls Your Name

*He called to her, "Mary"*
*And she heard her name,*
*She knew right then*
*Things would not be the same.*
*Christ had risen*
*He conquered the grave,*
*The message was clear*
*How God would save.*
*So whenever you feel*
*Lonely and afraid,*
*Afflicted with despair, weakness and shame,*
*Remember Yeshua always*

**For He called your name.**

## *<u>Take Me in Your Arms</u>*

*Take me in your Arms, Lord Jesus,*
*My master, my King.*
*For I am your bride,*
*Of your beauty I will sing.*
*You woo me with kindness, compassion and love,*
*Your hands touch me deeply to my heart*
*From above.*
*From above you reach down and embrace with your kiss,*
*Come take me to your chambers in Heavenly bliss.*
*Forever our hearts will beat as one,*
*For at the right hand of God you are seated with the Son.*
*I want us to be truly united as one,*
*Oh, this will be such sweet romance*
*When softly you whisper -*

**"Come my bride,**
**May I have this dance?"**

### Homesick for Heaven

Do you ever get homesick?
To go to our home someday with Him?
We shall see how beautiful it is
To be with Him...
It is the idea that our spirit is connecting with His.
Which makes it all so beautiful
To be with Him...
To see His face, gaze into His eyes,
Touch His hand.
Just to see how beautiful it is
To be with Him...
Eternal peace, everlasting Love
In unity we will live,

**Forever so beautiful
To be with Him.**

## <u>Seek First the Kingdom of God</u>

*If you seek first the Kingdom of God*
*You will find*
*That everything*
*Life has to offer shall be given*
*And defined.*
*Your purpose, your goals*
*He will help you attain.*
*From miracle to miracle His glory you will gain,*
*Because if you seek first*
*The Kingdom of God,*
*Everything else*
*Will come to you with Grace.*
*For it is only by His grace you are saved.*
*So seek ye first the Kingdom of God,*
*Seek His Work, His Heart, His Plan,*

**His Face.**

## <u>Strawberries from Heaven</u>

*They were plump, delicious, scarlet strawberries*
*Falling from Heaven.*
*Abundant fruit*
*Falling from Heaven.*
*Ripe, ready,*
*Already picked,*
*Abundant fruit falling from Heaven,*
*As red as a rose just for you.*

**Strawberries from Heaven**
**To refresh and renew.**

# Gods' Love for Yisrael (Israel):

*Genesis 17:7,8: I will establish My Covenant as an everlasting Covenant between Me and you and your descendants after you for the generations to come, to be your God and the God of your descendants after you. The whole land of Canaan, where you are now an alien, I give as an everlasting possession to you and your descendants after you; and I will be their God.*

## Together as One

The children of the world must be joined
Hand in hand,
Jew and Gentile
Throughout every land.
For each line and imprint
Upon every hand,
Forms an identifiable picture
Of Gods' wonderful plan.
Every fingerprint
Upon each person's hand,
Is carefully engineered
Into Gods' awesome plan.
Come let us be linked
Together as one,
Arm in arm, each tribe, with His Holy Son.
For we will join throughout every land,
We will soon be linked hand in hand.
Arise and go forth

**Children of Abraham.**

# **<u>Yisrael - The Jewels of My Kingdom</u>**

*I will gather them,*
*My precious gems.*
*Greatly valued and treasured,*
*Polished, refined, protected.*
*These are my precious jewels*
*They will gleam brightly*
*Outshine in the sun...*
*For in them my light flows through*
*Like laser beams, their light cuts deep -*
*Flows through like a raging river.*
*No one can deny or reject*
*Their beauty and splendor.*
*They catch the eye of man*
*And the heart of God*
*They are held in my hand*

**Yisrael- The Jewels of My Kingdom....**

## The Link

Israel,
The time has come to create a link.
One cannot form a chain without
A sturdy link
Between Jew and Gentile,
Nation to nation,
There must be a link.
Sturdy as a lion,
Tough like steel,
Pliable like the human heart,
I am your creator, the Potter, the Craftsman
Of His Handiwork.
We will join as a common link
With a common theme;
The most beautiful One,
We give Him Glory.
Onward we press
As we speak.
His Glory shall be made known
And prosper in His hand.
Gods' Glory will shine,
Christ's seed shall inherit
The Kingdom -
Link to link a chain is created.
Listen servants of the Lord,
Sons and daughters of Abraham,

**Let us climb.**

## The Gathering

Little lambs come to me
The shepherd He calls
Keep the flock together
So no one will fall.
Gather my lambs
The field is ready and the harvest is ripe
Sickles of copper and bronze
That blaze in the night.
Gather my lambs
Bring them in
The time is now.
Their light will no longer be dim
Like shining stars they shall go forth.
They shall go forth like stars,
Bright stars,
Morning stars…
Go forth like the dawn
Shining brightly -
The time is at hand
To gather my lambs.

**Your inheritance stands
Go gather my lambs.**

## <u>*Six points of a Star*</u>

*Do you not know there are six points of a star?*
*For God has created such a design*
*We can view from afar.*
*Each point He defines*
*Majestically intertwined,*
*The beauty of handiwork*
*Displayed for your eyes.*
*What does it mean these six*
*Points of a star?*
*It means that God took the time*
*To create and refine.*
*To show off His beauty*
*In all that we see,*
*Whether near or far.*
*These six points on a star*

**Show us how much more valuable**
**We truly are......**

# Gods' Covenant Promise:

## Yeshua Ha Mashiach (Jesus the Messiah)

*John 3:16:* For God so loved the world, that He gave His one and only begotten Son, that whoever believes in Him will not perish, but will have eternal life.

## Gods' Promise

No matter what happens,
I will still love you.
No matter what happens,
I will protect and renew.
Do not be afraid
And do not fear,
For I give you these comforting words
To your ear.
So even though trials may come to dismay,
Always know that I love you
You will not go astray...
For you know that there is
Neither death nor life
Nor Heaven nor hell,
Angels, demons or strife;
Height nor depth
Which can separate you
From My unfailing Love,

**Within my Son
Yeshua.**

## **_Isn't He Awesome?_**

Do you know we serve an awesome God?
Yes, we do.
An awesome God,
He spins planets within the galaxies,
He carefully adorns our flowers and trees.
He whispers, "I Love You", every day
A precious gift He sends our way.
We serve an awesome God with a mighty hand,
Who brings forth birth with a single command.
Who releases rain from storehouses on high
As the clouds constrict and drops fall from the sky.
He comforts the needy and provides for the poor,
He raises the lowly, like an eagle they'll soar.
He grants us His grace whenever we fail,
We know His mercy will always prevail.
We truly serve an awesome God.
Under the shadow of His wings we will forever abide,
With His righteous hand we will coincide.
No matter how busy our Creator on High,
He will always bend down to hear

**His childs' cry.**

## **_What is this mystery?_**

What is this mystery we call the Father's Love?
He was sent directly from Heaven above.
His loving tenderness embraces each one,
To those who receive Him and His Son.
The cornerstone of Salvation
When atonement began,
This mystery of Gods' wonderful love
Indeed, was sent from heaven above.
God is our Father and Christ His Son,
The Holy Spirit our Comforter
Since time has begun.
We are His children
Together, united as one,
This is a dilemma
Human reasoning cannot understand.

**From the beginning of time
It was part of God's plan.**

### __Burning desire__

Your heart burns into mine,
Mine into yours.
Deep within us
Exists a burning desire
To draw closer,
To be nearer.
The flame grows hotter -
Eternal flame,
Love everlasting.

**My burning desire......**

## **_From my heart_**

I shall be your comfort,
I shall be your strength.
I shall be your guide,
My grace, My peace, My Spirit is with you...
You will know from the beginning which
way to walk and which road to take.
I will light your path
Your footsteps will never be darkened
Never fade in the sand.
You will stand upright on Faith, or you will not stand....
For I am your Rock, your Refuge, your
Strength, your Joy, your Comfort-
I am your Song!
This song of life I give to you,

**My Precious Little Jewel......**

### The Covenant of God

*There is a promise I give to you Oh Israel.*
*There is a promise I give.*
*The rainbow of My Glory,*
*The colors of My Love,*
*I embrace you with My Covenant;*
*Beaming beauty,*
*Passionate Glory,*
*Everlasting Love,*
*Twisting and turning like a whirlwind*
*Circling around and around*
*The Star of David,*

**"The Branch of Jesse is shining."**

## *The Most Wonderful*

*He is the most Wonderful*
*God up above.*
*He is the most Powerful,*
*The Almighty God.*
*With love and tenderness*
*He tends to His flock,*
*With grace and mercy,*
*He gathers His lambs.*
*He answers on His time,*
*Not on our clock.*
*He holds us closely*
*In His mighty hands-*
*He is the most wonderful,*
*The Almighty God.*
*No matter what happens when we are down*
*When the waves come in*
*We will not drown,*
*So will His Love*
*Forever abound.*
*He is the most wonderful*

**God up above.**

## __The Boomerang of God__

Whatever goes out comes back to Him.
Any mission initiated by man,
Is tailored by God,
Is sent out by God and returns to God.
He accomplishes what he intended.
The lightning bolts report to Him;
They say, "Here we are",
His light returns to Him.
The wind goes out
And the wind returns,
Such as the Spirit of God
He sends forth His Love.
Which touches our hearts?
He proclaims us as His pride and joy
And praise returns to Him.
From our very lips
Which He created
Whatever goes out comes back to Him.
His Power, His Glory, His Majesty,

**The Boomerang of God!**

# The Symbol of the Tree

A tree is made of wood
And from the wood a fire starts,
And with this fire it burns
Within our very hearts.
Yeshua was nailed to a tree
And His children - we were set free.
The Kingdom of Heaven
Is much like that tree.
Where fruits are produced so abundantly,
Where the birds gather their young
And a new song is sung.
It was Yeshua, who hung on a tree
And ended all strife,
And like the Garden of Eden
He became our Tree of Life.
Is it really true that one who
Is hung on a tree is only a curse?
Well I myself question the words of this verse,
If that were true, then please tell me,

**Why is the Kingdom of Heaven
Compared to a tree?**

## **Dedication:**

*If this book has made an impression on your heart*
*You have an inner desire to ask Jesus the Messiah,*
*(Yeshua Ha Mashiach)- As your Lord and Savior,*
*Say this prayer:*

*"Lord Yeshua (Jesus), I need you.*
*Thank You for dying on the*
*Cross for my sins. I open the door of*
*my heart and receive you*
*As my Savior and Lord. Thank You*
*for forgiving my sins and*
*Giving me eternal life. Take control of my life.*
*Make me the kind of person you want me to be."*

*Now that you have received Yeshua (Jesus):*
*Yeshua has come into your life and heart*
*Your sins are forgiven*
*You became a child of God*
*You have received eternal life.*

*Exciting Daily changes to pursue in your "New Life":*
**Read Gods' Word daily,**
**Go to God in prayer daily,**
**Worship Yeshua/Jesus daily,**
*Anticipate the Holy Spirit to prompt*
*you moment by moment,*
*Witness for Christ by your life and words,*
*Trust God and ask the Ruach Ha Kodesh (Holy Spirit)*
*To empower your daily life.*
*Find a congregation of like minded believers in Christ.*

*"At the name of Jesus, every knee should*
*bend, in heaven and on earth,*
*And under the earth, and every tongue should confess that*
*Jesus Christ is Lord, to the Glory of God the Father."*

*Philippians 2:10-11*

*Date:* _____

## Heavens' Gold

*(Inspired Vision)*

*They were large sparkles of Gold,*
*Sprinkling down*
*Over my hands.*
*Shooting down*
*Like speckles of Gold*
*Particles of Gods' Love*

**Falling, falling, falling.....**

# __Shalom__

*As I was walking though the leaves*
*I wander slowly, shuffling my feet,*
*Gazing up high to the towering trees,*
*I say to myself*
*My God is complete.*
*He is thorough and grand,*
*In His nature He displayed*
*With a single command.*
*The foundation was laid*
*As a potter needs clay*
*From the eve to each morn*
*He began a new day.*
*A Covenant He made, upon a rainbow's bend*
*He is the Alpha, Omega, the Beginning and*
*The End.*
*His Love is clear, but sometimes discrete,*
*I say to myself*

**My God is complete.**

## _Blowing Snowflake Kisses to Heaven_

_There is nothing like His Love_
_So tender from above._
_My Heavenly Daddy_
_Holds me close like a dove._
_When He whispers my name_
_He forever proclaims_
_How wonderfully, fearfully_
_I am beautifully made._

_My desire to send Him_
_Snowflake kisses from my heart_
_Melts my Heavenly Daddy-_
_His Love won't depart._
_Blowing snowflake kisses to heaven_
_I shall always do_
_Because you are my Daddy_
_And I will always love you_...........

**_"Love Dawn"_**

# *MEDITATIONS:*

## <u>God predestined us to be His sons:</u>

*Romans 10: 12: "There is no difference between Jew and Gentile, the same Lord is Lord of all and richly blesses all who call on Him."*

# *With Just a Whisper*

_____

_____

_____

_____

_____

_____

_____

_____

_____

_____

_____

_____

_____

_____

_____

_____

_____

_____

_____

*Revelation 2: 17: "He who has an ear, let him hear what the Spirit says......to him who overcomes, I will give some of the hidden manna. I will also give him a white stone with a new name written on it, known only to him who receives it."*

# *With Just a Whisper*

_____

_____

_____

_____

_____

_____

_____

_____

_____

_____

_____

_____

_____

_____

_____

_____

_____

_____

_____

_____

_____

_____

_____

# *With Just a Whisper*

_____

_____

_____

_____

_____

_____

_____

_____

_____

_____

_____

_____

_____

_____

_____

_____

_____

_____

_____

_____

_____

_____

_____

## When He calls your name

_____
_____
_____
_____
_____
_____
_____
_____
_____
_____
_____
_____
_____
_____
_____
_____
_____
_____
_____
_____
_____

*Revelation: 20:15: "If anyones' name was not written in the book of life, he was thrown into the lake of fire."*

## *When He calls your name*

_____

_____

_____

_____

_____

_____

_____

_____

_____

_____

_____

_____

_____

_____

_____

_____

_____

_____

_____

_____

_____

## *When He calls your name*

_____

_____

_____

_____

_____

_____

_____

_____

_____

_____

_____

_____

_____

_____

_____

_____

_____

_____

_____

_____

_____

# *Take me in your arms*

_____

_____

_____

_____

_____

_____

_____

_____

_____

_____

_____

_____

_____

_____

_____

_____

_____

_____

_____

_____

*Isaiah 54:5: "For your Maker is your Husband-the Lord Almighty is His name- the Holy One of Israel is our Redeemer; He is called the God of all the earth."*

# *Take me in your arms*

---

# *Take me in your arms*

---

---

---

---

---

---

---

---

---

---

---

---

---

---

---

---

---

---

---

---

---

---

---

---

# Homesick for Heaven

_____

_____

_____

_____

_____

_____

_____

_____

_____

_____

_____

_____

_____

_____

_____

_____

_____

_____

_____

*1 Corinthians 15:51: "We will not all sleep, but we will all be changed, in a flash, in the twinkling of an eye, at the last trumpet. For the trumpet will sound, the dead will be raised imperishable and we will be changed."*

# *Homesick for Heaven*

_____

_____

_____

_____

_____

_____

_____

_____

_____

_____

_____

_____

_____

_____

_____

_____

_____

_____

_____

_____

_____

_____

_____

_____

_____

_____

# Homesick for Heaven

_____

_____

_____

_____

_____

_____

_____

_____

_____

_____

_____

_____

_____

_____

_____

_____

_____

_____

_____

_____

_____

_____

## *Seek first the Kingdom of God*

_____

_____

_____

_____

_____

_____

_____

_____

_____

_____

_____

_____

_____

_____

_____

_____

_____

_____

_____

_____

_____

*John 3:3-6: "I tell you the truth. Unless a man is born again of water and the Spirit, he cannot enter the Kingdom of God. Flesh gives birth to flesh, but the Spirit gives birth to Spirit."*

## Seek first the Kingdom of God

_____

_____

_____

_____

_____

_____

_____

_____

_____

_____

_____

_____

_____

_____

_____

_____

_____

_____

_____

_____

_____

_____

_____

# *Seek first the Kingdom of God*

_____

_____

_____

_____

_____

_____

_____

_____

_____

_____

_____

_____

_____

_____

_____

_____

_____

_____

_____

_____

_____

_____

_____

_____

_____

_____

# *Strawberries from Heaven*

_____

_____

_____

_____

_____

_____

_____

_____

_____

_____

_____

_____

_____

_____

_____

_____

_____

_____

_____

*Song of Songs 2:1: "I am a Rose of Sharon, a lily of the valley."*

# *Strawberries from Heaven*

_____

_____

_____

_____

_____

_____

_____

_____

_____

_____

_____

_____

_____

_____

_____

_____

_____

_____

_____

_____

_____

_____

_____

_____

## Strawberries from Heaven

_____

_____

_____

_____

_____

_____

_____

_____

_____

_____

_____

_____

_____

_____

_____

_____

_____

_____

_____

_____

_____

## Gods' Love for Yisrael (Israel):

*Ezekiel 43:2: "I saw the glory of the God of Israel coming from the east. His voice was like the roar of rushing waters, and the land was radiant with his glory."*

# Together as One

_____

_____

_____

_____

_____

_____

_____

_____

_____

_____

_____

_____

_____

_____

_____

_____

_____

_____

_____

_____

*Romans 10:12: "There is no difference between
Jew and Gentile - the same Lord is Lord of all
and richly blesses all who call on Him."*

# *Together as one*

_____

_____

_____

_____

_____

_____

_____

_____

_____

_____

_____

_____

_____

_____

_____

_____

_____

_____

_____

_____

_____

_____

_____

_____

_____

## Together as one

_____

_____

_____

_____

_____

_____

_____

_____

_____

_____

_____

_____

_____

_____

_____

_____

_____

_____

_____

_____

_____

_____

_____

# Jewels of My Kingdom

---
---
---
---
---
---
---
---
---
---
---
---
---
---
---
---

*Rev 21:18: "The wall was made of jasper, and the city of pure gold, as pure as glass. The foundation of the city walls were decorated with every kind of precious stone. The first foundation jasper, the second sapphire, the third chalcedony, the fourth emerald, the fifth sardonyx, the sixth carnelian, the seventh chrysolite, the eight beryl, the ninth topaz, the tenth chrysoprase, the eleventh jacinth, and the twelfth amethyst."*

# *Jewels of My Kingdom*

# *Jewels of My Kingdom*

---

# The Link

_____

_____

_____

_____

_____

_____

_____

_____

_____

_____

_____

_____

_____

_____

_____

_____

_____

_____

_____

*Galatians 3:26-29: "You are all sons of God through faith in Christ Jesus, for all of you who were baptized into Christ have clothed yourselves with Christ. There is neither Jew nor Greek, slave nor free, male nor female, for you all belong to Christ, then you are Abrahams' seed, and heirs according to the promise."*

# *The Link*

_____

_____

_____

_____

_____

_____

_____

_____

_____

_____

_____

_____

_____

_____

_____

_____

_____

_____

_____

_____

_____

_____

_____

_____

_____

_____

# *The Link*

_____

_____

_____

_____

_____

_____

_____

_____

_____

_____

_____

_____

_____

_____

_____

_____

_____

_____

_____

_____

_____

_____

_____

# The Gathering

---

*Zachariah 8:23: This is what the Lord Almighty says: In those days ten men from all languages and nations will take firm of one Jew by the edge of his robe and say, "Let us go with you, because we have heard that God is with you."*

# The Gathering

_____

_____

_____

_____

_____

_____

_____

_____

_____

_____

_____

_____

_____

_____

_____

_____

_____

_____

_____

_____

_____

_____

_____

# The Gathering

_____

_____

_____

_____

_____

_____

_____

_____

_____

_____

_____

_____

_____

_____

_____

_____

_____

_____

_____

_____

_____

_____

_____

_____

# *Six points of a star*

_____

_____

_____

_____

_____

_____

_____

_____

_____

_____

_____

_____

_____

_____

_____

_____

_____

_____

_____

_____

*Genesis 1:1: "In the beginning God created
the heavens and the earth."*

# *Six points of a star*

_____

_____

_____

_____

_____

_____

_____

_____

_____

_____

_____

_____

_____

_____

_____

_____

_____

_____

_____

_____

_____

_____

_____

_____

_____

# *Six points of a star*

## Gods' Covenant Promise:

### Yeshua Ha Mashiach (Jesus the Messiah)

*Revelation 1:8: "I am the Alpha and the Omega," says the Lord God, "who is, and who was, and who is to come, the Almighty."*

# Gods' Promise

_____

_____

_____

_____

_____

_____

_____

_____

_____

_____

_____

_____

_____

_____

_____

_____

_____

_____

_____

*Isaiah 9:6: "For to us a child is born, to us a son is given, and the government will be on His shoulders. And he will be called Wonderful, Counselor, Mighty God, Everlasting Father, and Prince of Peace."*

# *Gods' Promise*

_____

_____

_____

_____

_____

_____

_____

_____

_____

_____

_____

_____

_____

_____

_____

_____

_____

_____

_____

_____

_____

_____

_____

_____

_____

_____

# Gods' Promise

_____

_____

_____

_____

_____

_____

_____

_____

_____

_____

_____

_____

_____

_____

_____

_____

_____

_____

_____

_____

_____

## *Isn't He awesome?*

_____

_____

_____

_____

_____

_____

_____

_____

_____

_____

_____

_____

_____

_____

_____

_____

_____

_____

_____

_____

_____

_____

_____

*Revelation 1:8: "I am the Alpha and the Omega, says the Lord God, who is, and who was, and who is to come, the Almighty."*

# *Isn't He awesome?*

_____

_____

_____

_____

_____

_____

_____

_____

_____

_____

_____

_____

_____

_____

_____

_____

_____

_____

_____

_____

_____

_____

# Isn't He awesome?

_____

_____

_____

_____

_____

_____

_____

_____

_____

_____

_____

_____

_____

_____

_____

_____

_____

_____

_____

_____

_____

_____

_____

_____

# What is this mystery?

_____

_____

_____

_____

_____

_____

_____

_____

_____

_____

_____

_____

_____

_____

_____

_____

_____

_____

*Isaiah 53: 3-12: "He was despised and rejected by men, a man of sorrows....... He was pierced for our transgressions, he was crushed for our iniquities; the punishment that brought us peace was upon him, and by his wounds we are healed. .......he bore the sin of many, and made intercession for the transgressors."*

## *What is this mystery?*

_____

_____

_____

_____

_____

_____

_____

_____

_____

_____

_____

_____

_____

_____

_____

_____

_____

_____

_____

_____

_____

_____

_____

_____

# What is this mystery?

_____

_____

_____

_____

_____

_____

_____

_____

_____

_____

_____

_____

_____

_____

_____

_____

_____

_____

_____

_____

_____

_____

_____

_____

_____

# *Burning Desire*

 

---
---
---
---
---
---
---
---
---
---
---
---
---
---
---
---
---
---
---
---

*Isaiah 41:10: "Fear not for I am with you, be not dismayed*
*for I am your God, I will strengthen you and help you:*
*I will uphold you with my righteous right hand."*

# *Burning Desire*

_____

_____

_____

_____

_____

_____

_____

_____

_____

_____

_____

_____

_____

_____

_____

_____

_____

_____

_____

_____

# *Burning Desire*

_____

_____

_____

_____

_____

_____

_____

_____

_____

_____

_____

_____

_____

_____

_____

_____

_____

_____

_____

_____

_____

_____

# *From My Heart*

_____

_____

_____

_____

_____

_____

_____

_____

_____

_____

_____

_____

_____

_____

_____

_____

_____

_____

_____

_____

_____

_____

*Isaiah 30:21: "Whether you turn to the right or to the left, your ears will hear a voice behind you, saying: This is the way, walk in it:"*

# *From my heart*

_____

_____

_____

_____

_____

_____

_____

_____

_____

_____

_____

_____

_____

_____

_____

_____

_____

_____

_____

_____

_____

_____

## From my heart

_____

_____

_____

_____

_____

_____

_____

_____

_____

_____

_____

_____

_____

_____

_____

_____

_____

_____

_____

_____

_____

_____

_____

_____

# The Covenant of God

_____

_____

_____

_____

_____

_____

_____

_____

_____

_____

_____

_____

_____

_____

_____

_____

_____

_____

_____

*Isaiah 42:6: "I, the Lord, have called you in righteousness: I will take hold of your hand. I will keep you and will make you to be a covenant for the people and a light for the Gentiles."*

# The Covenant of God

# The Covenant of God

_____

_____

_____

_____

_____

_____

_____

_____

_____

_____

_____

_____

_____

_____

_____

_____

_____

_____

_____

_____

_____

_____

_____

# The Most Wonderful

_____

_____

_____

_____

_____

_____

_____

_____

_____

_____

_____

_____

_____

_____

_____

_____

_____

_____

_____

*Proverbs 25:2: "It is the Glory of God to conceal a*
*matter, to search out a matter is the glory of Kings."*

# *The Most Wonderful*

_____

_____

_____

_____

_____

_____

_____

_____

_____

_____

_____

_____

_____

_____

_____

_____

_____

_____

_____

_____

_____

_____

# The Most Wonderful

_____

_____

_____

_____

_____

_____

_____

_____

_____

_____

_____

_____

_____

_____

_____

_____

_____

_____

_____

_____

_____

# The Boomerang of God

_____

_____

_____

_____

_____

_____

_____

_____

_____

_____

_____

_____

_____

_____

_____

_____

_____

_____

_____

_____

_____

_____

_____

_____

*Mark 4:41: They were terrified and asked each other; "Who is this? Even the wind and the waves obey him!"*

# The Boomerang of God

_____

_____

_____

_____

_____

_____

_____

_____

_____

_____

_____

_____

_____

_____

_____

_____

_____

_____

_____

_____

_____

_____

_____

# *The Boomerang of God*

_____

_____

_____

_____

_____

_____

_____

_____

_____

_____

_____

_____

_____

_____

_____

_____

_____

_____

_____

_____

_____

_____

_____

_____

## The Tree

---
_____

_____

_____

_____

_____

_____

_____

_____

_____

_____

_____

_____

_____

_____

_____

_____

_____

_____

*Deuteronomy 21:22-23: "If a man is guilty of capital offense is put
to death and his body hung on a tree, you must not leave his
body on the tree overnight. Be sure to bury him that same day,
because anyone who is hung on a tree is under Gods' curse."*

# *The Tree*

_____

_____

_____

_____

_____

_____

_____

_____

_____

_____

_____

_____

_____

_____

_____

_____

_____

_____

_____

_____

_____

_____

_____

_____

## *The Tree*

### Prayer Meditation

*Deuteronomy 6: 4-9: "Hear O Israel: The
Lord our God, the Lord is one.
Love the Lord your God with all your
heart, soul, mind and strength.
These commandments that I give you
are to be on your hearts.
Impress them on your children. Talk
about them when you sit at home,
when you walk along the road, when you
lie down and when you get up.
Tie them as symbols on your hands and
bind them on your foreheads.
Write them on the doorframes of your
houses and on your gates."*

# Heavens' Gold

---

---

---

---

---

---

---

---

---

---

---

---

---

---

---

---

---

---

---

*Matthew 2:11: "Coming to the house, they saw the child with his mother Mary, and they bowed down and worshiped him. Then they opened their treasures and presented him with gifts of gold and of incense and of myrrh."*

# Heavens' Gold

_____

_____

_____

_____

_____

_____

_____

_____

_____

_____

_____

_____

_____

_____

_____

_____

_____

_____

_____

_____

_____

_____

# Heavens' Gold

_____

_____

_____

_____

_____

_____

_____

_____

_____

_____

_____

_____

_____

_____

_____

_____

_____

_____

_____

_____

_____

_____

_____

# *Shalom*

_____

_____

_____

_____

_____

_____

_____

_____

_____

_____

_____

_____

_____

_____

_____

_____

_____

_____

_____

_____

*Psalm 37:37: "There is a future for the man of peace."*

# *Shalom*

_____

_____

_____

_____

_____

_____

_____

_____

_____

_____

_____

_____

_____

_____

_____

_____

_____

_____

_____

_____

# *Shalom*

---

---

---

---

---

---

---

---

---

---

---

---

---

---

---

---

---

---

---

---

---

---

---

## Blowing Kisses to Heaven

_____

_____

_____

_____

_____

_____

_____

_____

_____

_____

_____

_____

_____

_____

_____

_____

_____

_____

_____

*Isaiah 40:11: "He tends his flock like a shepherd: He gathers the lambs in his arms and carries them close to his heart: He gently leads those that have young."*

# *Blowing Kisses to Heaven*

---

## Blowing Kisses to Heaven

_____

_____

_____

_____

_____

_____

_____

_____

_____

_____

_____

_____

_____

_____

_____

_____

_____

_____

_____

_____

_____

_____

# Dawn Rose Brekke R.N.

*Dawn grew up in the Metropolitan
area of Detroit, Michigan and
Had a love for writing beginning in
elementary school years to the present.*

*Dawn is a Registered Nurse for 30 years.
Successfully graduated from the U.S. School
of Aerospace Medicine as a Distinguished
Graduate, and served 4 years in the
United States Air Force. Her performance
of service was in Military Intelligence and
Decontamination/Chemical Warfare training.*

*Dawn has a daughter Kristal,
Son in law Mark along with being an
ecstatic grandmother of two beautiful
grandchildren, Belle and Jacob.*

*Dawn has been born again since January
2001 and has received many inspirational
writings from the Ruach Ha Kodesh. The
greatest opportunity she has ever had, is
the wonderful and blessed opportunity
to serve her Father in Heaven and
Messiah Yeshua, her Lord and Savior.*

*This is all done through none other than the power of His Holy Spirit!*

*Kadosh, Kadosh, Kadosh.*
*Yeshua Ha Mashiach.*

## Annette M. Rousseau, RN, MBA

### (AKA-Renee Grace)

Annette grew up in the Metropolitan area of Detroit, Michigan and has been an RN over 20 years. Annette is also known as Renee Grace which is her signature name for Trademarked handmade jewelry called Streets of Gold Jewels®.

It can be found on Etsy.com under Streets of Gold Jewels as well as an exclusive artist shop in Sedona, Arizona named Adonai. Email: reneesog@yahoo.com (www.Adonaichristianfineart.com)

Annette has known Dawn since she was born again in January, 2001. Dawn was touched by the Ruach Ha Kodesh and has had supernatural moments of inspiration and impartation from the Ruach Ha Kodesh.

These writings are from the only author- The Ruach Ha Kodesh.

Dawn was and continues to be a prayer and worship instrument and accepted these words from the Alpha and the Omega.

Much Love to the Ruach Ha Kodesh:

# STREETS OF GOLD JEWELS ®

**Mission** – *Deliver quality, customized, affordable signature jewlery as a piece of art.*

**Vision** – *Every Queen of the Earth have a customized mothers' or birthstone bracelet or necklace made exclusively for her. Present the city of the New Jerusalem as art in jewelry. (Rev. 21: 18)*

**Philosophy of Life** – *Work hard, play hard and live a healthy, happy life and bless as many people possible along the way. Isaiah 29: 12: "All that we have accomplished He has done for us."*

**Jewelry line:**
*1. The New Jerusalem Jewelry: necklaces and bracelets:*
*2. Mothers' bracelets and necklaces at request:*
*3. Rainbow bracelets and necklaces at request.*
*Primary stones used: Fresh Water Pearls and Swarovski Pearls. Birthstone Swarovski Crystals; Gemstones.*

**New Jerusalem Jewelry: Streets of Gold Jewels ®**
*Origin: Revelation 21: 18-21(NIV)*
*18 The wall was made of jasper, and the city of pure
gold, as pure as glass. 19 The foundations of the city
walls were decorated with every kind of precious stone.
The first foundation was jasper, the second sapphire,
the third agate, the fourth emerald, 20 the fifth onyx, the
sixth ruby, the seventh chrysolite, the eighth beryl, the
ninth topaz, the tenth turquoise, the eleventh jacinth,
and the twelfth amethyst.21 The twelve gates were
twelve pearls, each gate made of a single pearl.
The great street of the city was of gold,
as pure as transparent glass.*

**Each New Jerusalem piece:**

*12 pearls with at least one stone of:*
*Jasper*
*Chrysoprase*
*Sapphire*
*Chalcedony*
*Emerald*
*Amethyst*
*Beryl*
*Sardonyx*
*Chrysolite/ Peridot*
*Carnelian*
*Topaz*
*Jacinth*

**Mothers' bracelets/birthstone bracelets: Swarovski crystals:**

Jan- Garnet
Feb- Amethyst
March- Aquamarine
April- Diamond
May- Emerald
June- Alexandrite/Pearl
July- Ruby
August- Peridot
Sept- Sapphire
Oct- Opal
Nov- Topaz
Dec- Tanzanite

**Rainbow Line:**
Bracelets and Necklaces made from Swarovski crystals:
Buyer may choose silver or gold base
as well as both if requested.
Red
Orange
Yellow
Green
Blue
Indigo
Violet

**Proprietor and originator of Trademark:**
Annette Marie Rousseau, (AKA: Renee Grace)
reneesog@yahoo.com

## Streets of Gold Jewels® is officially Trademarked by the USPTO.

# *Other Recommended Leadership Resources:*

Dish Network:
Sid Roth- It's Supernatural – Messianic Jew
Joseph Prince
Joel Osteen
Joyce Meyer
The Jewish Jesus- Messianic Jew
Jonathan Bernstein- Messianic Jew

Internet Resources:
Bill Johnson
Eagles Wings- Ministry to the Jewish People
David Herzog Ministries- The Glory Zone- Messianic
Joshua Mills
Bobby Connor
Todd White

Dr. William Wong NPHD- Essentials of Natural Health:
(Naturopathic Medicine: lecture, podcasts, products)

Printed in the United States
By Bookmasters